in Situ

Mark English Architects

in Situ
Unique Homes Crafted for California Living

CONTENTS

7   An Architecture of Place
by Zahid Sardar

11   Meadow House

41   Tōrō

61   Silicon Valley

83   Atherton

113   Cow Hollow

137   Lighthouse

157   Terrace House: A Process Case Study

176   The Office

177   Acknowledgments

178   Project Credits

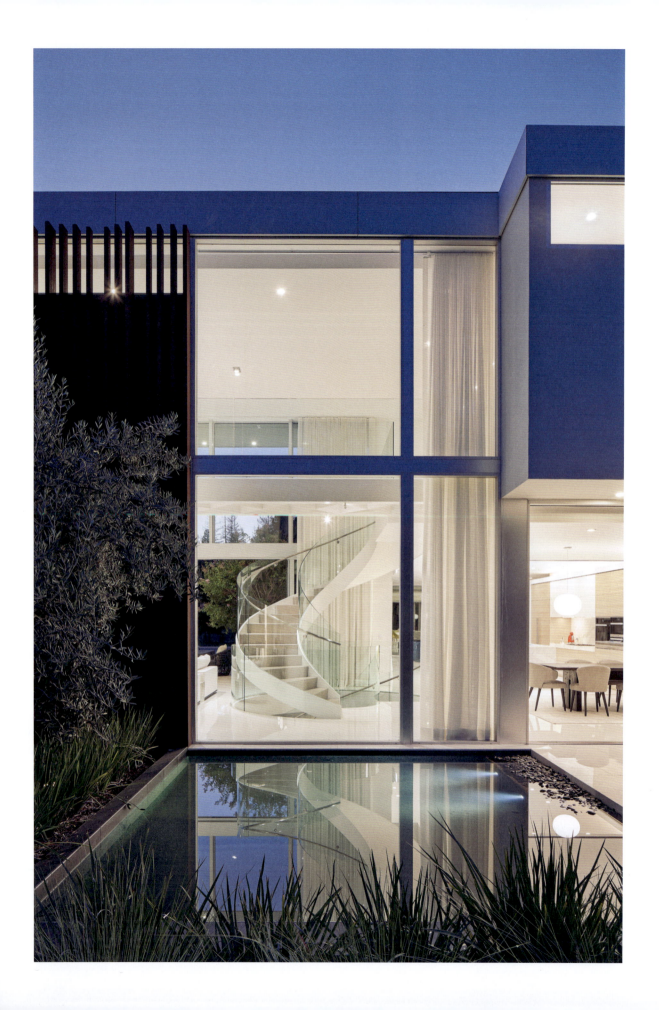

AN ARCHITECTURE OF PLACE

By Zahid Sardar

Zahid Sardar, the editor-in-chief of *SHLTR™ magazine*, is a San Francisco-based writer specializing in architecture, interiors, and design. He has authored many design books, curated exhibitions, and was the *San Francisco Chronicle*'s design editor for two decades. His work also appears in *The New York Times*, *Dwell*, and other publications.

A house rises in a setting, in a period of time, and is thus a receptacle of living culture.

These three aspects—place, time, culture—form the essence of 'site' and this has been the foundation for San Francisco architect Mark English's design philosophy throughout his career, which spans more than three decades and over 300 homes.

Seven of these homes in northern California, selected for this book, offer a tour of his work—ranging from his latest projects to older ones, including one still in progress. These homes illustrate the process Mark follows, which often begins with consulting a landscape architect to create site-specific designs that honor diverse locations, from expansive open spaces to more constrained existing footprints.

This prolific architect's fascination with land and architecture began early. "I was always interested in examining the land," Mark recalls, remembering summer trips with his family from the San Francisco Bay Area, where they lived, to upstate New York, where they were from. These trips often passed through Joshua Tree National Park, where he would forage for arrowheads and other treasures. This connection to the land was deepened by visits to New Mexico, Arizona, and Utah, where the ruins of pueblo cities made a lasting impression. Hopi homes, built with earth-based materials in geometric grids that followed the land's contours, inspired his vision of architecture as a response to its environment.

Mark also found inspiration in his family's collection of *National Geographic* magazines, which introduced him to ancient cities like Cusco and the Maya civilization. At age ten, he copied a drawing of a Maya building and, in doing so, 'discovered' the laws of perspective and vanishing points. This epiphany sparked a lifelong passion for architecture. Later, when he visited those same ancient sites, he saw how the Inca had modified their environment by clearing the land—a lesson in how not to approach site design. He prefers, like the Hopi, to work with the land, rather than altering it drastically.

Mark's first serious foray into the art of building was as a nineteen-year-old in San Jose, where he partially built a house that he had designed. "When you see your building being framed, it captures you," he says. This early experience led him to pursue an undergraduate architecture degree at Cal Poly, where he also worked in construction. He went on to earn a master's degree from the Syracuse University School of Architecture in Florence, where he developed a passion for field-study excursions. One memorable trip took him atop Rome's ancient Pantheon, home to the world's largest unreinforced concrete dome. "Few people get to do that. It opened up another world of architecture," Mark says.

When he returned to California, Mark was inspired by the works of architects Stanley Saitowitz and Mark Mack. He experimented with airbrush drawing techniques they had developed and, after working for others in San Luis Obispo and San Francisco, opened his own firm, Mark English Architects, in 1992.

Mark's approach to architecture is rooted in the belief that "nature comes first, then human nature." His designs prioritize the site over the program, acknowledging the land's role in shaping the built environment. A prime example of this philosophy is his work at the Santa Lucia Preserve in Carmel Valley, a 20,000-acre conservation land trust with just 300 designated spots for homes. Of the roughly 150 homes already built, **Meadow House**, the first of Mark's four projects there, stands as an award-winning model.

The Preserve stretches from Carmel Beach to the mountains eastward, and within that terrain are redwood groves, grasslands, high desert lands, hot springs, and snow-covered peaks. Each site is different. Situated within this landscape, close to the main lodge, the house follows the topography and acknowledges the movement of wildlife, its low, screened buildings creating a seamless connection between indoors and outdoors. "The home follows the path of birds, the movement of animals, and the fragility of plant species around it," Mark says.

Another example is **Tōrō**, a home near Woodside that borders forests and feels remote. Built above a riparian landscape of second-growth redwoods, the southern side of the home borders a forest of deciduous oaks, cottonwoods, and willows. Between these distinct areas stands a unique double-trunked redwood tree that serves as a symbolic totem. The home's design takes advantage of the surrounding landscape, with the owner's favorite space—the dining room—opening to expansive views of this tree.

Mark's work is also evident in a 1960s home in **Silicon Valley**. The original structure was constrained by its existing design, but Mark found a way to improve its views by creating a cantilevered deck off the north end. New steel posts and modern materials allowed for wider openings, and a new elevator made the home fully accessible. In this case, Mark didn't drastically alter the architecture; instead, he improved it by enhancing the connection to the landscape.

In **Atherton**, Mark's design of an H-plan home integrated his client's Asian cultural values with the site's characteristics. The flat, undistinguished 1-acre lot presented a challenge, but Mark responded with distinctive elements based on feng shui principles. A Corten steel screen facade symbolizes 'entropy,' while a long-lived olive tree in the front garden offers balance. Inside, a fireplace wall made of book-matched veined quartzite evokes an ink drawing of a sacred mountain, and a dramatic curved staircase circulates 'chi' energy throughout the open-plan space.

In San Francisco's **Cow Hollow** district, Mark transformed a 1917 Shingle-Style building into a modern home, retaining the exterior's historic envelope while completely overhauling the interior. The once dark, compartmentalized spaces were opened up to allow more light and views. Skylights now flood the interior with natural light, offering views of the sky and the surrounding cityscape. "The cityscape offers a new perspective," Mark notes.

In Sausalito, Mark worked on a quirky 1980s hexagonal house called **Lighthouse II** that sat at the base of a hill and was partially supported by a pier. The original design, with its faceted roof and nearly windowless walls, was disconnected from its spectacular views. Mark's solution was to open up the house by adding steel framing and large glazing panels, effectively 'stitching' the home to the view.

The final project, **Terrace House**, in Woodside, illustrates Mark's process in action. Located on a 3-acre site that was initially considered unbuildable due to its steep slope and past use as a hunting location, the land had to be reimagined. Mark envisioned a multilevel home cascading down the hill, each level providing flat rooftops that would double as terraces. This design not only made the steep site usable but also provided stunning views of neighboring sculpture gardens and the rolling ocean fog. Nearly completed, the Terrace House includes an indoor pool, a guest pavilion with a pool on top, and extensive outdoor spaces. "If this was ever a tussle between site and program," Mark says, "consider it a draw."

Mark English's work demonstrates that architecture is not just about buildings; it's about responding to the land and its history, while also accommodating the needs of its inhabitants. In his homes, site and program are inseparable, each enhancing and informing the other, always synchronized.

MEADOW HOUSE

Meadow House presented us with an opportunity to work within the exceptional Santa Lucia Preserve in the Carmel Valley. Both the site and brief paved the way for a challenging and, ultimately, deeply rewarding process.

The brief from our clients—a multigenerational family with business ties to their native Korea—outlined a Californian home with a Korean heart. Exploring these singular influences revealed many similarities, all of which can be seen throughout Meadow House, from the fluidity of indoor-outdoor spaces and deep terraces surrounding parts of the home, to the abundance of natural light that is overt in some places and tempered in others.

Interestingly, 90 percent of the preserve is protected by a conservation land trust and as a result, there are only a few hundred dwellings within this vast, unruly landscape. Those privileged enough to build here must follow strict design and development guidelines to protect the natural ecologies and inherent beauty of this place. For example, tree and plant species must be left untouched, and any built contribution must be predominantly undetectable from surrounding roads, trails, and public spaces.

For this reason, siting the home within the meadow was complex and our response is defined by a Z-shaped form that follows the contours of the land, reaching out in some places and yielding in others. The gently sloping topography and dense oak canopies work together to conceal the residence from passersby, and the weathering steel and cedar cladding approximate the colors of the natural environment, further dissolving the boundaries between built form and landscape.

Alongside the composite of Californian and Korean sensibilities, our clients wanted to be able to conduct business at home; entertain large groups of people—both for work and personal purposes; and host family members for long and short stays. Our response to this is deliberate in its conception but subtle in experience, allowing for a residence that is simultaneously generous and intimate. The sense of volume is palpable with wide corridors and sweepings ramps (our dignified response to accessibility requirements and the clients' wish to age in place) yet private areas are noticeably quieter. Finally, views are omnipresent, and a palette of Italian bluestone, white oak, cedar, quartz, and stainless steel brings depth to the internal experience.

For us, one of the most exciting elements of this project is the sunken lounge at the tip of the living pavilion. Not long after the project's completion, we spent an afternoon lazing in this cozy recessed spot, where the glow of the sun indirectly warmed the space and cast a golden hue. Through the open doors of the living room, we watched the local wildlife forage in the long grasses, and indulged in the untouched beauty of the surrounding landscape.

This is just one anecdote from a deeply meaningful project, and Meadow House's resonance is the sum of many parts, including the sun-soaked terraces, quality of light, and proximity to nature. Given its complexities, we see it as a delightfully distilled contribution to Carmel Valley's incomparable landscape.

Physical and digital models greatly assist in the development of projects. With both, the opportunity to study the form from multiple viewpoints is invaluable and gives both the designer and owner insight into the end experience of the building. During the design process, computer modeling allows for careful analysis of sun and shadow studies at any point of the day and any day of the year, while a finished physical model helps to grasp the scope of work in an expeditious and complete way. Both model making techniques help to promote ideas toward built reality.

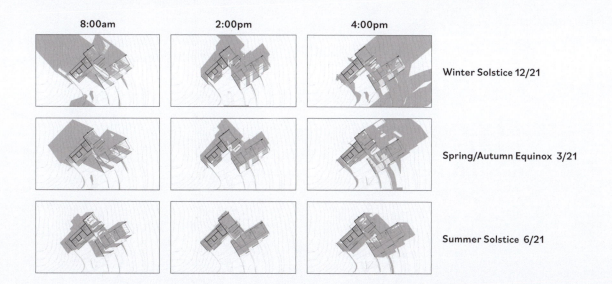

Site plan
02 8 16 24 40

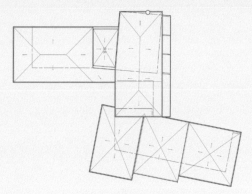

Roof plan

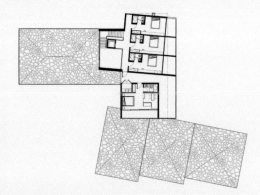

Second-floor plan

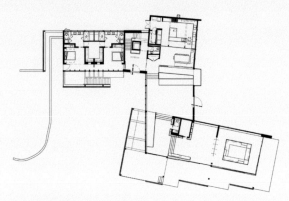

First-floor plan

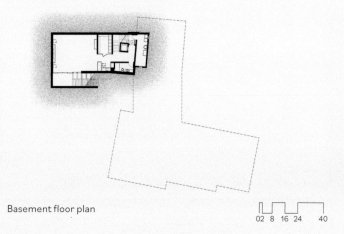

Basement floor plan

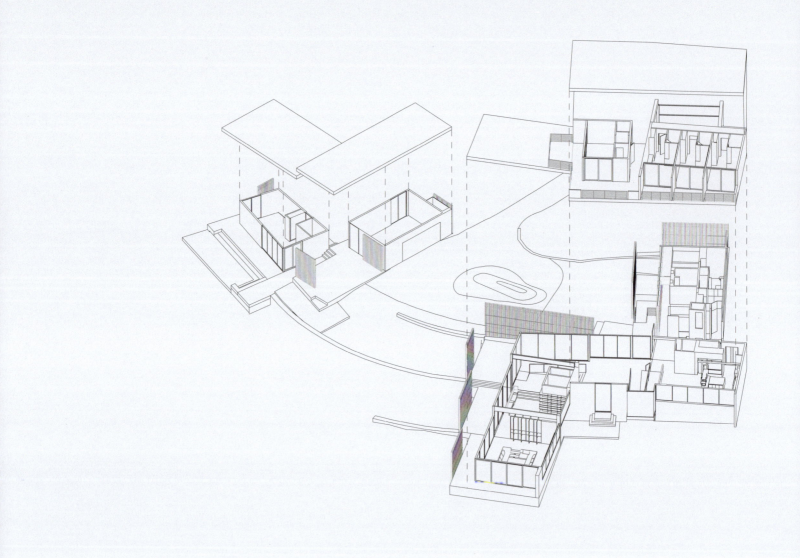

TŌRŌ

For this project, we were engaged by the client to renovate and extend an existing 1950s-era home on a sloping site in Woodside. Bookended by a forest to the east and a deciduous grove to the west with a majestic redwood tree at its periphery, the Tōrō residence's appealing setting and mid-century bones were central to our design response.

From the outset, our endeavor was to create a home that added the necessary program and accentuated the feeling of being perched above the ground in the canopy of redwoods. Our client—a product designer, software engineer, and playwright whose hand can be found in several well-designed products many of us encounter every day—brought his affinity for craft and love of Japanese design ideals to the project. In addition, he was drawn to the choreography of the house and therefore it was integral that we maintain its essence while increasing the footprint and enhancing the program.

Alongside these considerations, our scope of work was directly influenced by the 50-foot setback requirements imposed across the site. Thankfully, the existing L-shaped home and garage preceded these setbacks, consequently extending into them, and the new rectangular extension containing the dining area and office space sits within the buildable area at the center. Connected to the existing via a central hallway, the new is pragmatic in plan and joyful in experience thanks to a careful consideration of massing and volume.

Given the sloping site, the arrival sequence begins at street level where a stairway crafted from a series of granite slabs leads visitors to a canopied entrance deck wrapping a Japanese garden. This quiet planted space, which abuts the mature redwood stretching through the site, offers a formative moment of tranquility and repose, setting the tone for the entire project. From this vantage point, the new and old can be considered in tandem and the juncture between the two is intentionally subtle—an effect enhanced by the cantilevered roof planes that nod to the home's modernist roots and strengthen the form's rectilinear nature. Crucially, these deep eaves also control solar penetration and create transitional indoor-outdoor spaces fitting for the climate.

Our intention to create a consolidated form was also greatly facilitated by the materiality. Aside from a series of glass doors that retract completely, opening the home to the surrounding landscape, the exterior is clad almost entirely in clear, finished cedar, echoing the timber decking underfoot. The cedar siding wraps the eaves, extending onto the ceilings of the dining room and office spaces, creating visual continuity and material cohesion that helps to amalgamate the form. In contrast, the remainder of the interior palette is crisp with white finishes, teak accents, and muted porcelain and travertine-tiled floors. The client's furniture, artwork, and objects enliven the spaces, as do views to the surrounding trees.

In many ways, Tōrō is a study of harmonious dualities; Japanese and mid-century sensibilities comingle and old and new forms converge. These dichotomies are omnipresent yet never jarring, giving this home its enduring identity and, most importantly, offering our client a renewed place of refuge among the redwoods.

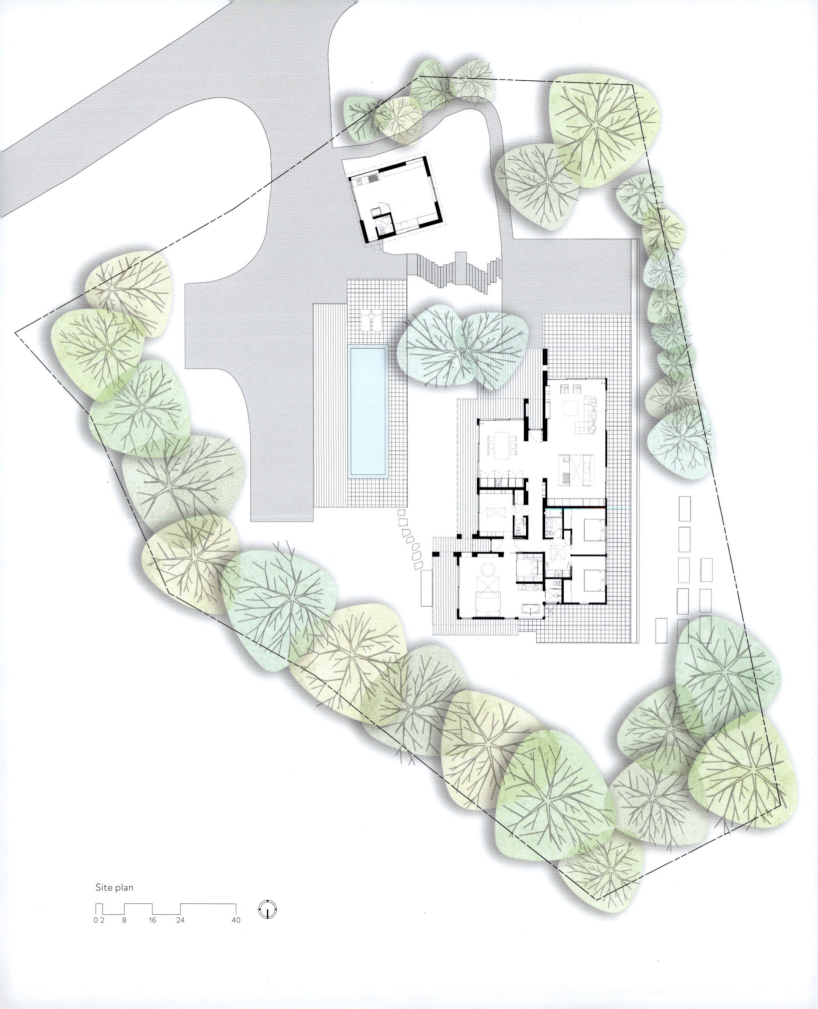

Site plan
0 2 8 16 24 40

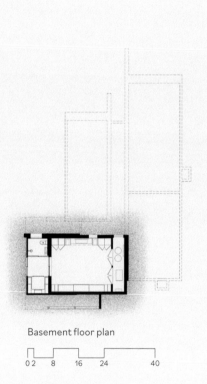

Basement floor plan

0 2 8 16 24   40

First-floor plan

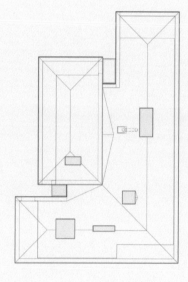

Roof plan

Developing early study sketches and models assisted the process of realizing the distinct and elegant form of the Tōrō residence. The appearance of the simple massing and sequence of living spaces belies the fact of a carefully considered arrangement on this unique wooded site.

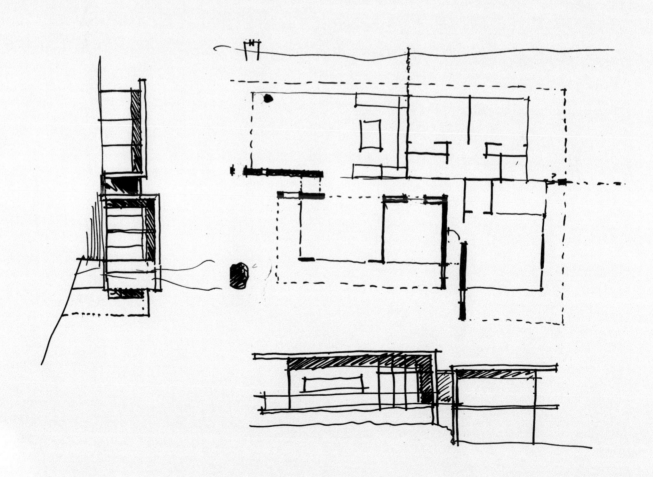

SILICON VALLEY

This project encompassed a renovation and addition to an existing mid-century hillside home in Silicon Valley. With incredible aspects and good bones, the home was promising yet poorly realized, and we set out to elevate it through a thoughtful and intuitive reworking.

The existing form possessed many great qualities; we admired the audacity of the soaring roof shape and cantilevered deck, which would've been considered daring at the time, but ultimately the home lacked finesse in its materiality and flow. Consequently, we didn't expand the envelope, except to add an elevator connecting the new garage to the main floor so that our clients could age in place, as well as enclose the open-air space below the main living area with an automated sliding-glass-door system. Alongside these additions, we focused on bringing cohesion to the design, leaning heavily on modern technology to create fluidity across the plan and improve thermal mass.

Unifying the exterior wall finishes was key to achieving a sense of harmony. Cedar siding now wraps the home, its horizontal arrangement enhancing the rectilinear nature of the form without adding visual cutter. Complemented by double low-E glazing and highly reflective fixed glass panels, which work to reduce solar heat gain, and enveloped by the surrounding vegetation, the form retains its modernist character with newfound subtlety.

The interiors are similarly pared back with a palette of timber, glass, and concrete. White-oak flooring and cedar ceilings bring warmth, and cast concrete pavers in the living space and adjoining cantilevered terrace create continuity between indoor and out. There are bright and playful moments, too, thanks to sporadic injections of color.

Firstly, the full-height cast glass entry window, which is an important original feature. Comprising an abstract geometry of glass in shades of red, blue, green, and yellow, it's a fine example of arts and crafts in architecture and a rare decorative element we were determined to retain. Further, in the kitchen, burnt-orange lacquered cabinets pick up the warm tones of the reclaimed eucalyptus veneer felled at the Presidio in San Francisco, making for a feature both punchy and visually easy to digest.

We also incorporated cold-rolled steel as a foil to the earthiness of the timber. In the entry, full-height sheets of steel with a water-jet-cut perforated wave pattern and adjustable hued LED lamps—conceived as a modern nod to the original cast glass entry window—encase a low seat, providing a moment to pause or remove your shoes. The wave theme is echoed in the in situ painting by Momoko Sudo in the living room. Also, steel reappears here as the fireplace surround, this time hot-rolled and with naturally occurring fabrication marks.

Many of these custom and artfully conceived details were influenced by our clients—two seasoned technology founders with a no-nonsense style and a love of mid-century architecture. Their interest in modern technology, well-made furnishings, and industrial design surely enriched our response, and it was incredibly fulfilling to explore their many varied affinities through the built form.

Site plan

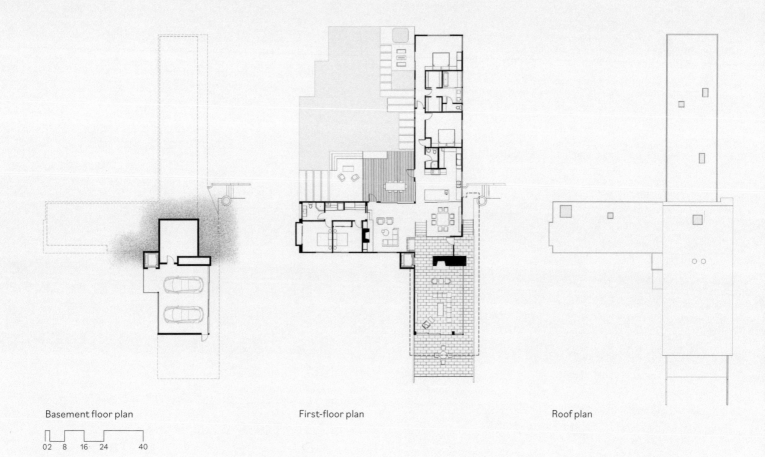

Basement floor plan

First-floor plan

Roof plan

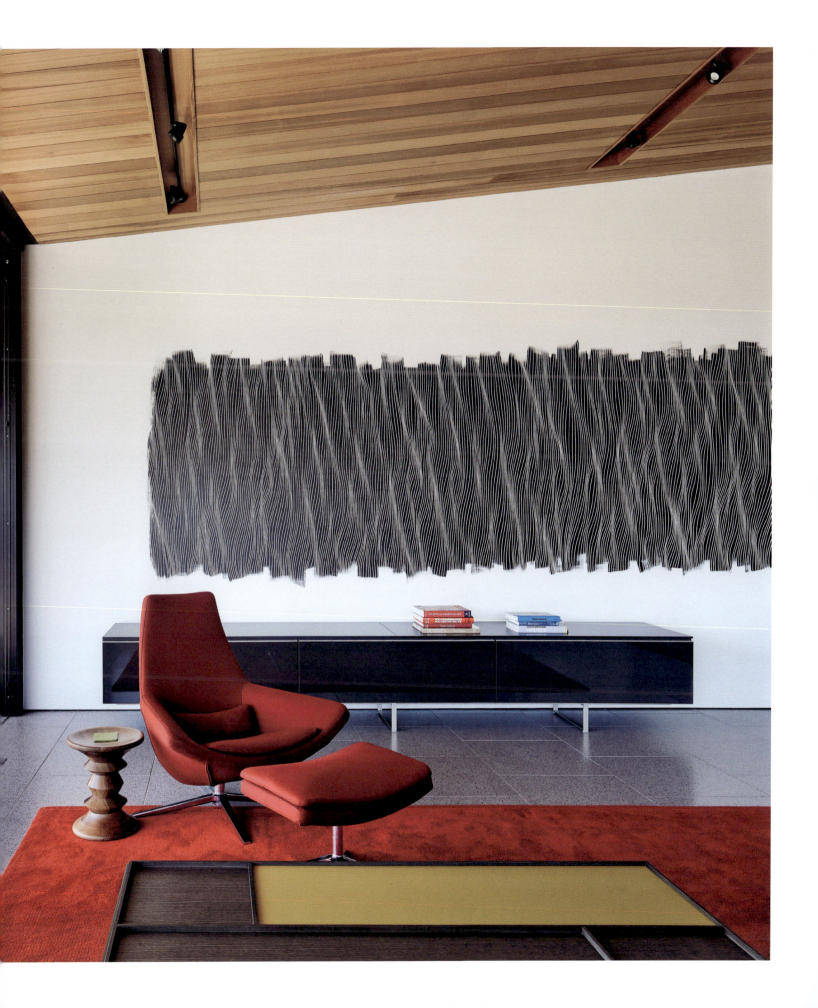

Many disparate design elements came together to form a cohesive expression of individual taste in the Silicon Valley residence. A sense of craftsmanship, from the existing refurbished solar/wind shades and stained-glass entry side light to the new in situ painting and cold-rolled-steel fireplace finish, permeates the completed remodel. Each component was carefully considered to generate an appearance pure in materiality and refined in fabrication.

ATHERTON

Atherton is a large family home for a professional couple and their two teenaged children. Conceived as a place of comfort and amenity as well as one of joy and wonder, Atherton provided us with an opportunity for creative exploration through a domestic lens.

For our clients, who both work in the tech industry, this project represented the beginning of a new chapter in California. Having resided and built homes in Singapore and Hong Kong, they were well versed in the intricacies of designing a home, and approached us with a clearly defined brief. Our ensuing goal was to create a residence that embraced its Californian context and responded to our clients' family dynamic.

Located on a 1-acre site with similarly sprawling neighboring lots, we designed the house as a classic H-plan encompassing a pair of two-story wings connected via a double-height space. The two wings provide a sense of enclosure and privacy along the property's northern and southern boundaries, containing the everyday experience of the home yet facilitating a distinct feeling of openness across the site. Further, the form allows for alcoves of the yard to be embraced by the mass of the building, creating protected pockets of outdoor space as well as carefully composed sightlines that traverse the site as opposed to into neighbors' properties.

We conceived the internal layout in collaboration with a feng shui expert who was engaged by the clients to provide advice on finishes and furnishings, as well as on how configurations affected the flow of energy into the home. The central pavilion, which contains the double-height living area, is the home's nexus and a welcoming communal space. At the northern end, a custom fabricated staircase

crafted from steel and glass corkscrews through the void space, leading to the upper level and down to the basement lounge below. Above, an acrylic-and-steel bridge traverses the void from left to right, connecting the two wings and making a bold visual statement overhead. Notably, there is an element of theatrics here as human movement animates the architecture, introducing a hint of playfulness and nuance to the highly pragmatic plan.

On the upper level, the southern wing contains three bedrooms with bathrooms whereas the northern wing is dedicated entirely to a generous primary suite with a bedroom and adjoining robe and bathroom. There is also a private roof terrace to the west that overlooks the pool and courtyard below. Back on the ground floor, the northern wing unfurls to the rear of the property, containing the dining room, kitchen, and a secondary living room. These shared ground floor spaces express an overt connection to the backyard where paved and green areas surround the pool and a sense of effortlessness feels front of mind.

Though highly defined in its geometric form, there is an atmosphere of fluidity to Atherton that nods to the clients' patterns of use and to the home's locality. Pleasingly, the form and its series of carefully conceived spaces facilitate the type of Californian lifestyle our clients initially sought and have since emphatically embraced.

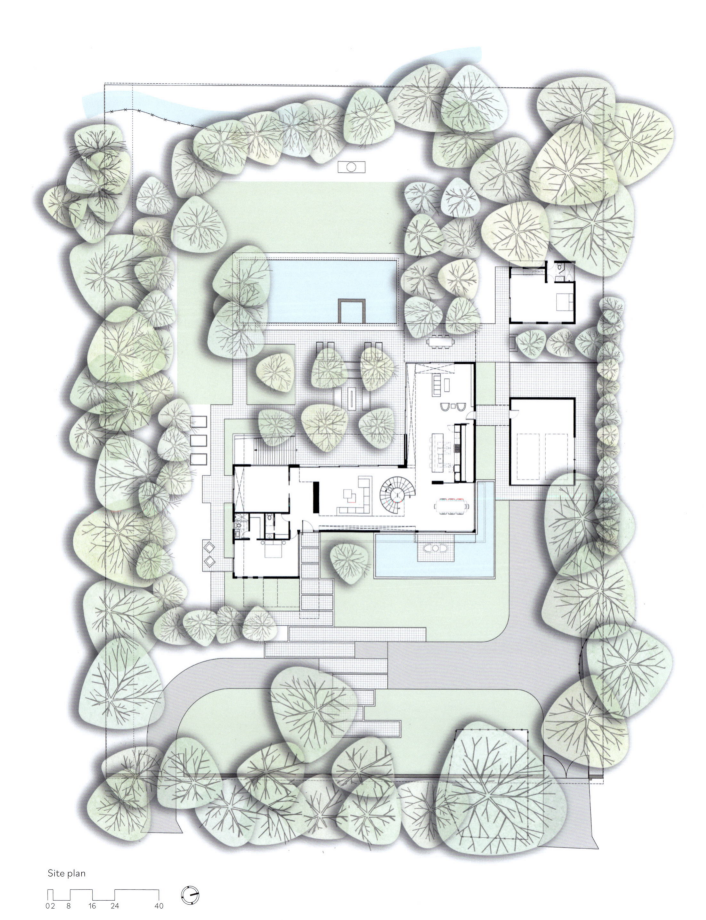

Site plan
0 2 8 16 24 40

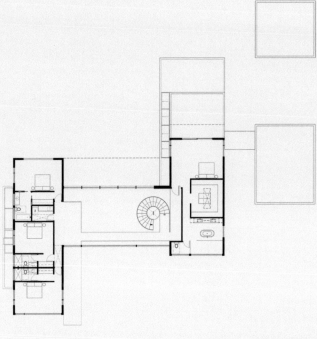
Second-floor plan

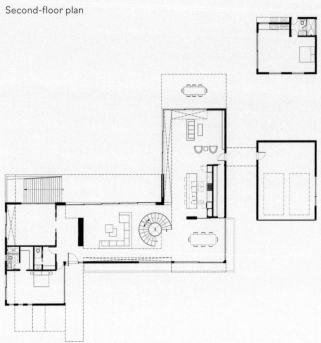
First-floor plan

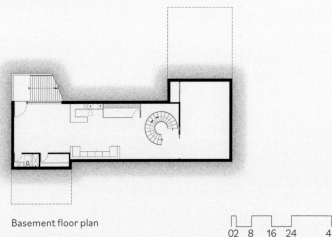
Basement floor plan

 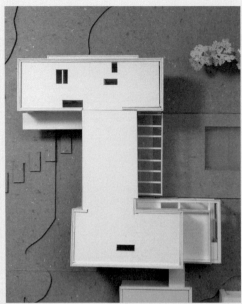

A principal method of architectural form making is the creation of physical study models. There is an immediacy in understanding both the design opportunities and the objectionable pieces requiring further reworking. Each successive model builds on the last, forming a direction toward the spatial solution.

This methodology was in no small way utilized in the shaping of the Atherton residence. The shifting and cantilevering of model program pieces helped determine the eventual direction and form of the home.

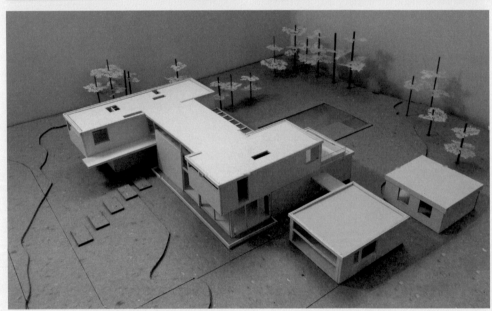

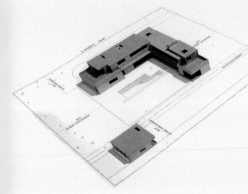 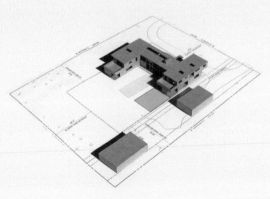 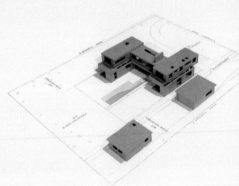

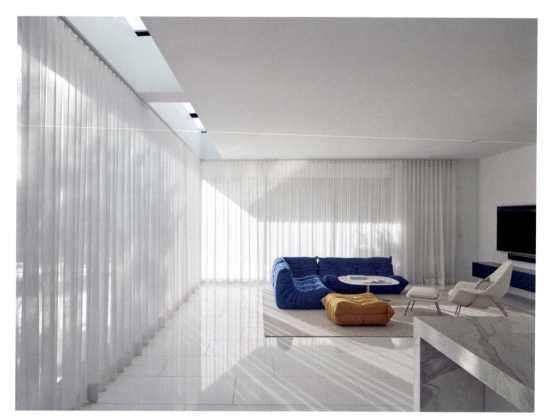

The two-story interior stair was an opportunity to introduce an expressive curving element within the rectilinear volumes of the Atherton residence. Working closely with the steel fabricator to coordinate the installation and finish, the stair turns upward connecting the three levels with an elegant sweep of steel and glass. The result is a moment of light into the lowest level and a dramatic instance of vertical circulation within the home.

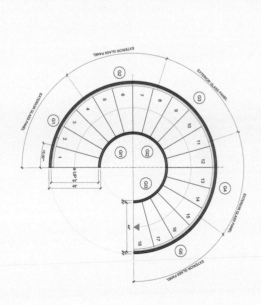

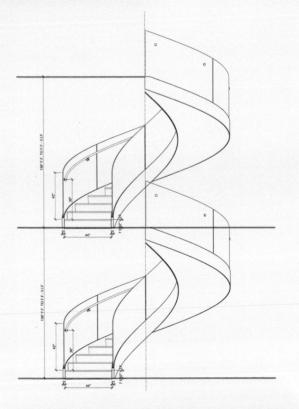

COW HOLLOW

This project encompassed a remodel and a small addition to an existing two-story family home in San Francisco's Cow Hollow neighborhood. Originally designed in 1917 by architect Elizabeth Austin—one of a small handful of American women architects working in the early twentieth century—it was an honor to be tasked with protecting her vision while ushering the residence into a new époque.

Cow Hollow's original design displays many elements of the Arts and Crafts movement as well as the First Bay Tradition, a local adaptation of the popular East Coast Shingle Style. These influences can be seen in the wood shingle siding, brick chimney, asymmetrical facades, varied eave lines, and numerous roof gables, which give the building its distinctive charm and gravitas.

As a historically significant building, it is protected under a landmark preservation scheme that demanded special planning review, historic analysis of the existing building and proposed changes, and public engagement. This process, paired with our own ambition to retain the building's architectural identity and celebrate Austin's work, heavily guided our design response. This included meticulously restoring the facade (during the construction process, every piece of external ornament was removed, labelled, and reinstated) and conceiving a series of thoughtful interventions and additions that would enrich the existing structure.

Inside, we reimagined the layout to facilitate a more contemporary way of life for our clients. As well as converting existing crawl space to habitable square footage and making additions at the first and second levels, we completely opened up the central part of the U-shaped plan. Here, we removed most of the second floor, creating

a double-height dining space at the heart of the home. A cantilevered steel-and-glass staircase wraps the room and a new skylight above floods the void with natural light, emulating the feeling of an atrium. While this bold design move decreased the home's square footage, it undoubtedly enhances the quality of the space and reveals the home's innate grandeur.

The materiality is intended to feel relevant and modern but also fitting for the home's heritage. Glass, metal, and wood are crisp and unfussy—a reflection of our casual and unpretentious clients—and dark, rough-sawn wood floors bring warmth. There are also notes of blond bamboo in the cabinetry and interior window frames, which are new but fabricated in the same size and shape as the originals. With several skylights throughout, including in the primary bathroom, the quality of light is brilliant and views to the garden and surrounding trees brighten the interiors, creating a sense of serenity despite the urban locale.

It is our hope that this home pays deference to its lineage while embracing its newness. We believe architects should be concerned with how people live, and this home, which has effortlessly traversed generations as a beautiful and functional place to live, is our interpretation of that philosophy.

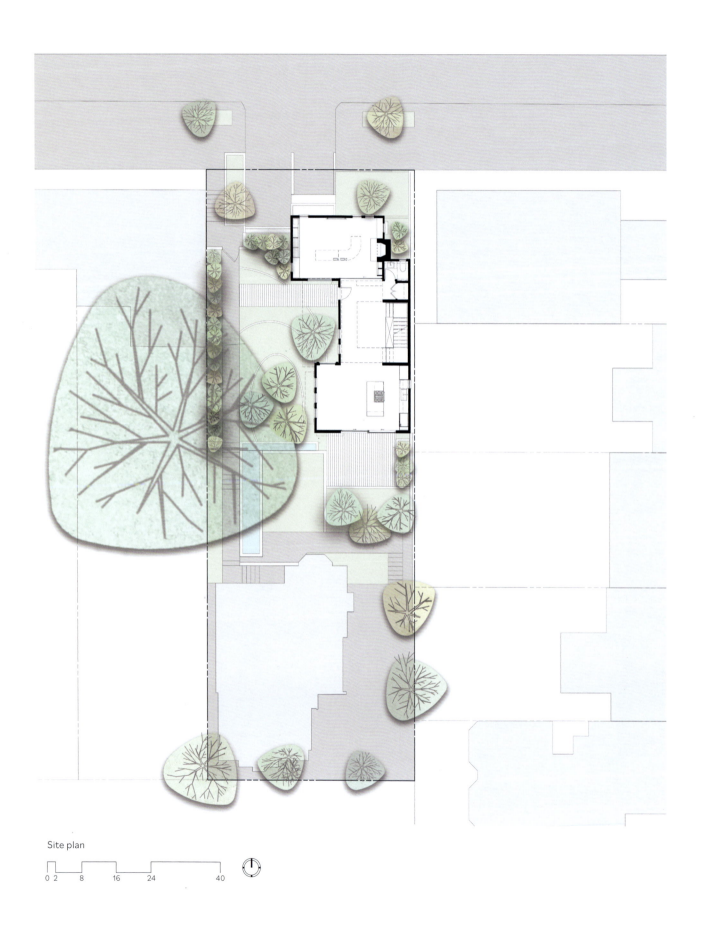

Site plan
0 2 8 16 24 40

Basement floor plan

First-floor plan

Second-floor plan

Roof plan

0 2 8 16 24 40

With limited floor space available for a dining room, the owners requested the design of a minimum footprint/fold-away type table that occasionally could accommodate up to six guests while also having the ability to downsize to a side table.

Preliminary, small-scale paper models helped lead to the bespoke solution of a simple double flip-out wood tabletop over a double pivoting steel base. The straightforward concept required the precise steel and wood craftsmanship of Andrew Williams of IronGrain in Oakland, California who brought the design into reality. The walnut tops, with interlocking finger joint hinges at the edges, were threaded together with stainless-steel pin rods that, when brought to the fully open position, made a completely flush surface. The simplicity of the design and fine fabrication made for an elegant solution meeting the owners' needs.

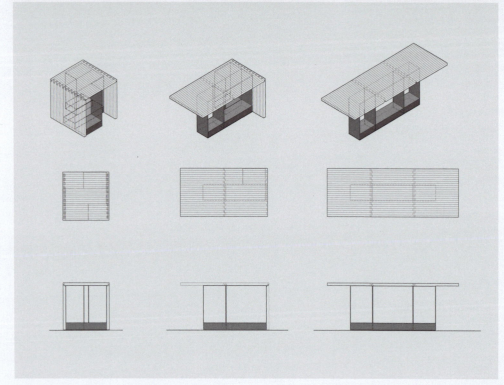

In opening up the central area of the home to light and creating a greater sense of volume, the importance of designing the main stair to share this feeling of lightness became apparent. Cantilevered steel risers and landings elevate the experience of traveling to the upper floor steel-framed bridge. Connecting the upper bedrooms, the bridge design, with its opaque acrylic walkway and tempered glass railing set in black steel, adds a surprising brightness to the space as light from the large central skylight illuminates the walking surface. Along with the cantilevered stair, the winding circulation path around the central space delivers a notable engineering presence into the heart of the home.

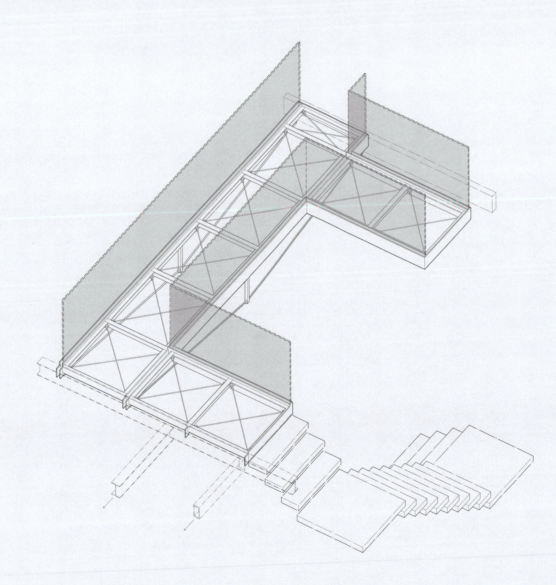

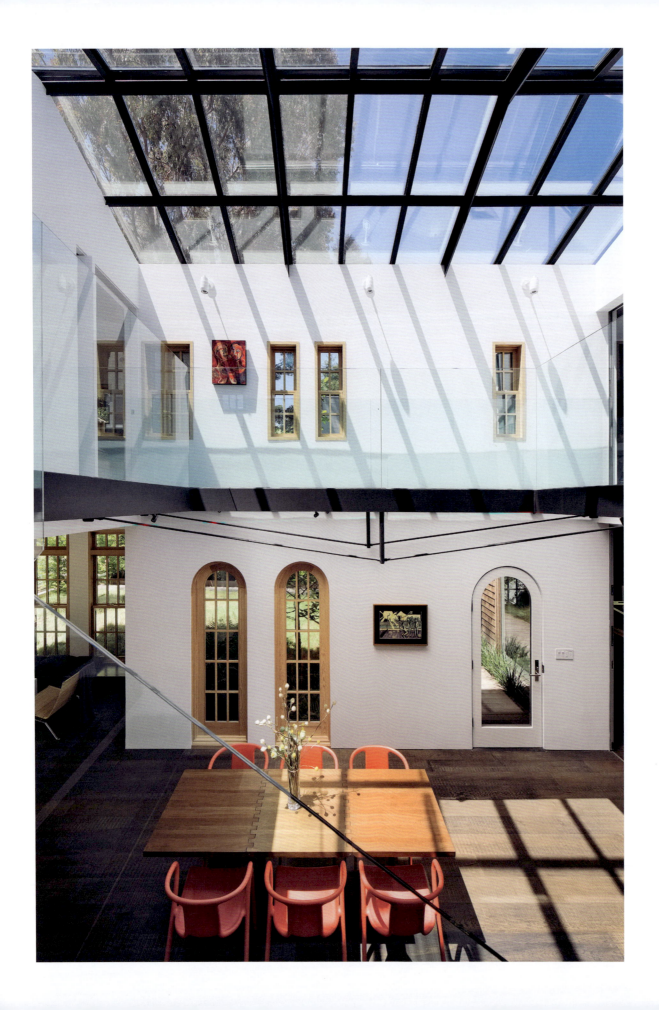

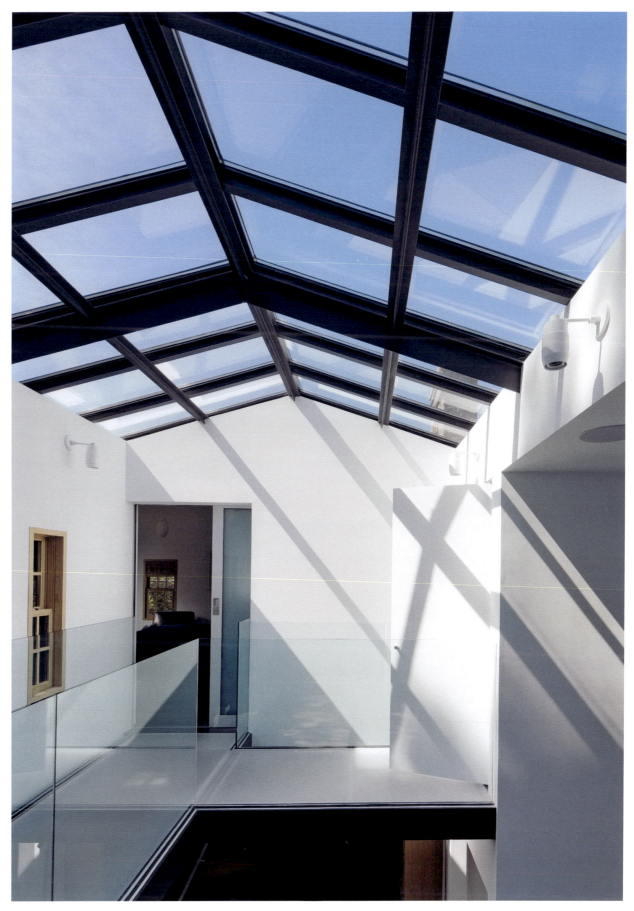

LIGHTHOUSE

Lighthouse is a single-family residence at the foot of a hill overhanging San Francisco Bay. With views to Angel Island and Alcatraz Island, the waterfront Sausalito home held great appeal to us and our clients, and maintaining its essence guided our design response alongside a pursuit for increased openness and light.

Our clients, a New York–based couple, had previously lived in a Sausalito home designed by our firm. Given this familiarity, they engaged us to introduce a sense of artistry and intention to their next home, Lighthouse. As avid collectors and keen supporters of the arts, their brief outlined a dramatic place to live among their treasured pieces when visiting from Manhattan.

The existing dwelling is uniquely north Californian, drawing on a variety of influences including the local self-built houseboats and alternative homes typical of the 1960s and 70s. Designed by local architect Kirk Hillman in the mid-1980s, it is one of a pair of unusual houses perched at the water's edge, dubbed Lighthouse I and Lighthouse II. Our clients were drawn to the latter for its unrivalled siting and distinctive character, particularly its intricately designed hexagonal floorplan that pinwheels upward three levels to a crow's nest.

Given the home's location in a seismically active zone, we replaced the existing timber frame with structural steel—a process that required significant consultation with a structural engineer. Another notable challenge pertained to the steep topography and limited site access. One of the area's quintessential tram cars ferries the residents and their visitors to and from street level; however, an alternative method was required for construction traffic. The answer lay in a barge that

transported all materials and finishes including timber, steel, concrete, and all demolition debris to and from the site via its private dock.

Inside, the home retains its offbeat charm through the jagged floor plan and changing ceiling heights. We were determined to celebrate its quirkiness; however, the roof configuration limited the size and location of picture windows, and several interior walls obstructed views. As a result, we removed a series of walls to allow for a more fluid layout and raised the eaves to create space for floor-to-ceiling windows that capture generous aspects to the water and San Francisco's skyline in the distance.

The new steel frame is exposed in places, introducing an element of industrial cool, and our clients' dynamic collection of modern art and mid-century furniture brings a vibrant energy. We believe the most powerful upshot, however, is this home's newfound sense of light and aspect—a notion that not only invigorates the everyday experience of Lighthouse but makes sense of its desirable location.

Site plan

02 8 16 24   40

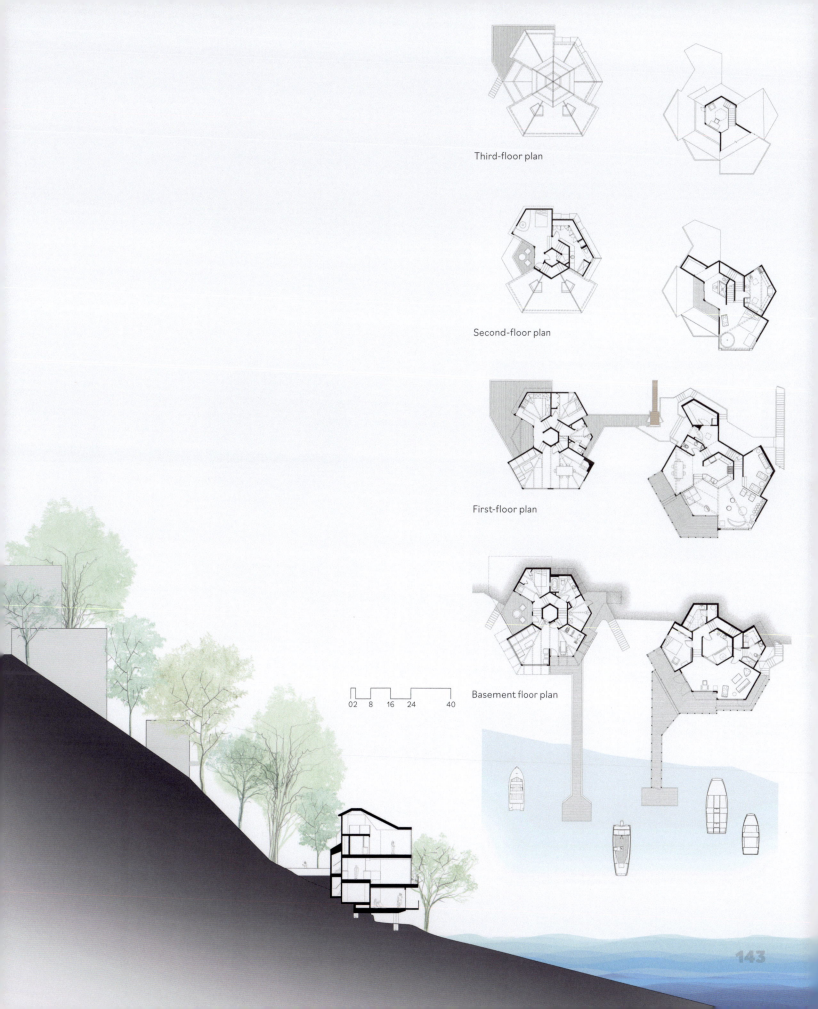

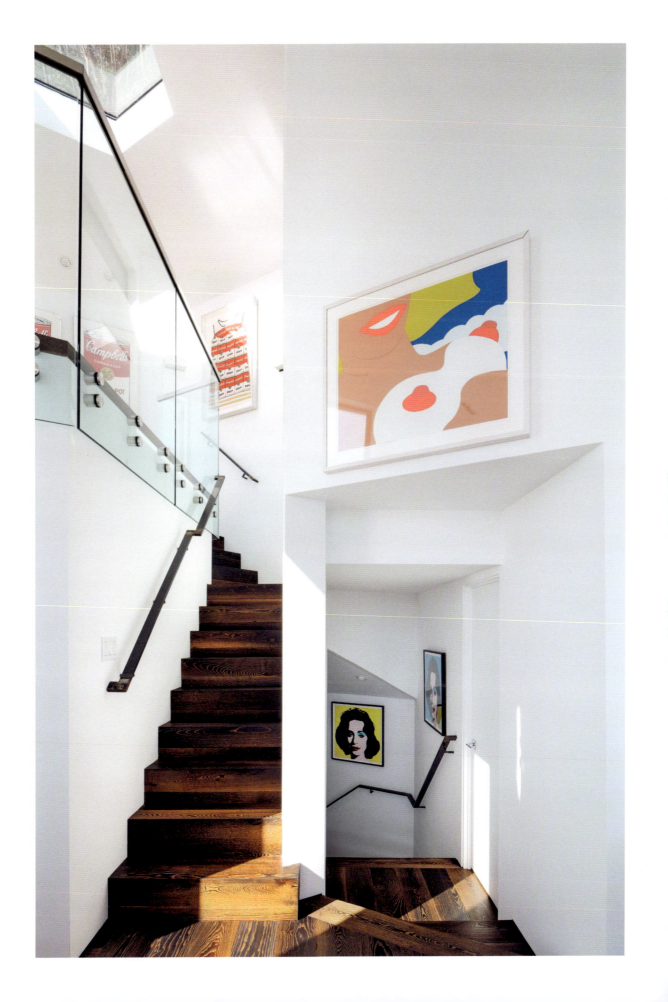

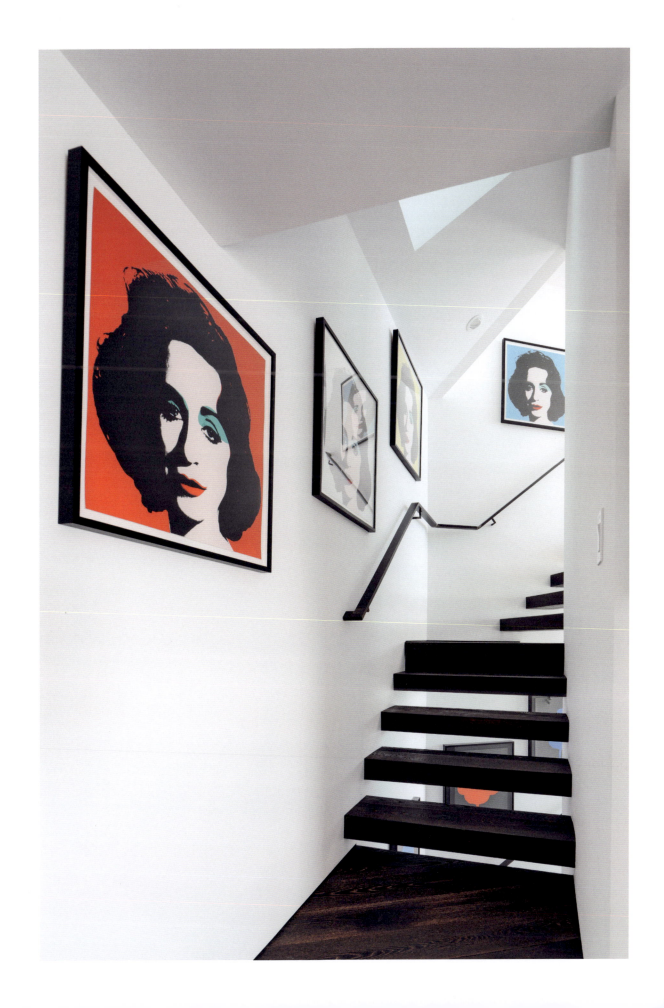

TERRACE HOUSE
A PROCESS CASE STUDY

The successful development of any good building is grounded in a nuanced process.

It ultimately begins with the owner; one of their first steps is to select an architectural team whose input will not only guide the design rationale but define how it will function. The builder is also essential, and a compelling collaboration between the architect, owner, and builder is the foundation of any great project.

The process is deeply involved. From initial site visits and sketching to permitting and construction, it encompasses many complexities and unknowns. To this end, it takes cooperation, vision, time, patience and, perhaps most importantly, courage.

The following pages illustrate the process for Terrace House. As we progressed from design development to construction, we engaged additional consultants whose dedication and insights greatly contributed to bringing Terrace House to life smoothly and efficiently.

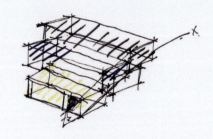

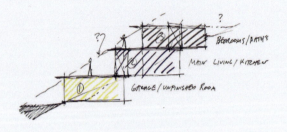

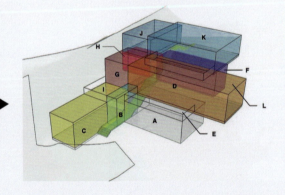

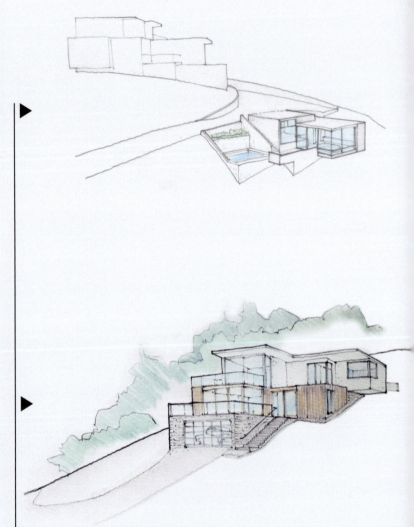

INITIAL SKETCHES + BLOCK DIAGRAMS IDEAS

Starting the process of taking the owner's ideas of living, and moving them toward a built form, one must consider the restriction of the site, budget, and time all while considering the opportunities of the site and building program. After initial site visits and design discussions, diagrams and initial sketches form the building blocks upon which ideas can grow. As preliminary proposals are viewed and agreed upon, ideas are moved forward to further development of the vision and intent of the building.

DESIGN DEVELOPMENT SKETCHES

Hand drawings are essential tools to help develop initial design ideas. Quick sketches may lead to discovering an early understanding of how the building form should relate to the site and surroundings.

2020

PHYSICAL MODEL

The building of physical models is helpful on a number of levels. One might argue that there is no tool that can convey the ideas of massing and relationship to the site as effectively as a model. The ability to hold up, look into, and imagine the development of the design ideas into reality is the advantage that a model brings to the design process.

159

3D STEEL STRUCTURAL MODEL

Digital visualization tools not only help present how the building will look to the owners but can also assist in the conversation with consultants and the builder on assembly and detail. Creating a digital model of the proposed steel structure for the Terrace House helped not only convey the work of the structural engineer within the architectural form but also discover potential conflict areas that may not have been realized until construction.

2021

3D STRUCTURAL MODEL

The ability to visualize a building's complete structure from multiple perspectives is a great advantage in communicating design ideas to the owner and the builder. Quantities of site excavation work and how the foundation sits on the site are understood in a more succinct manner. The work of the structural engineer is brought together with that of the architectural form resulting in an understanding of building components and their relationships.

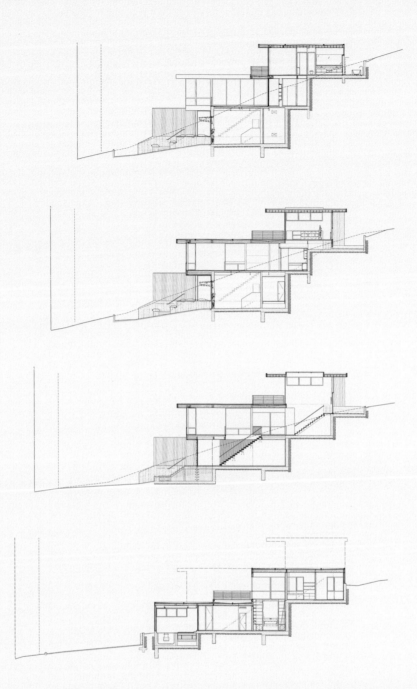

BUILDING DEPARTMENT SUBMISSION DRAWINGS

Building cannot begin without approvals from the authorities having jurisdiction and these approvals cannot be granted without a measured and coordinated construction drawing set. The architectural design ideas formed through presentation and dialogue with the owners are brought together with the structural and civil consultant work to create the instructions for building. A safe and environmentally sound structure are fundamental goals and the creation of a well-constructed drawing set is at the heart of a successful building.

2021

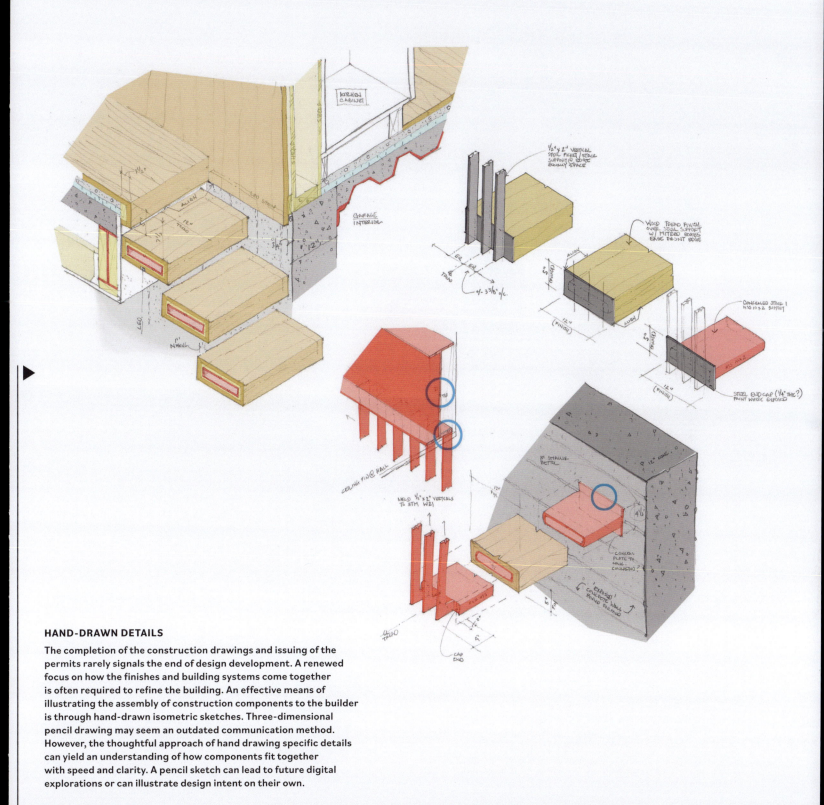

HAND-DRAWN DETAILS

The completion of the construction drawings and issuing of the permits rarely signals the end of design development. A renewed focus on how the finishes and building systems come together is often required to refine the building. An effective means of illustrating the assembly of construction components to the builder is through hand-drawn isometric sketches. Three-dimensional pencil drawing may seem an outdated communication method. However, the thoughtful approach of hand drawing specific details can yield an understanding of how components fit together with speed and clarity. A pencil sketch can lead to future digital explorations or can illustrate design intent on their own.

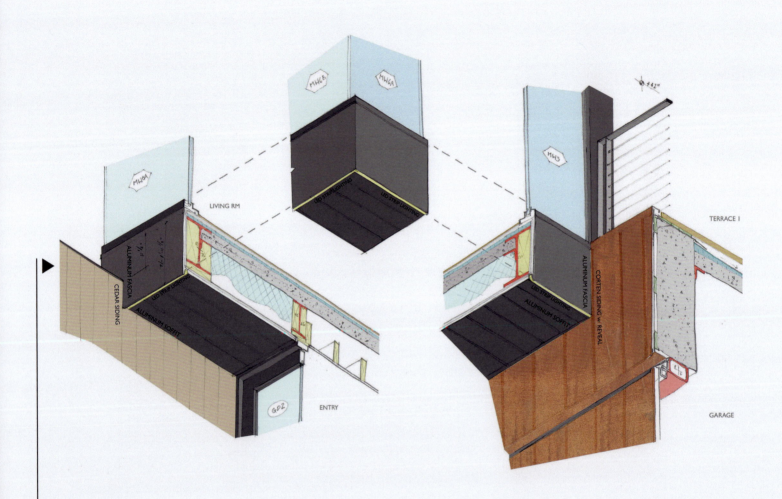

HAND-DRAWN DETAILS

There are many moments in a building's design where the different components coming together require a 3D drawing to understand and convey the finished intent. To help facilitate this understanding, computer graphics are important, but hand drawing can be equally valuable in this process. A practiced hand in graphically constructing details is also a good tool to take to the job site.

2021

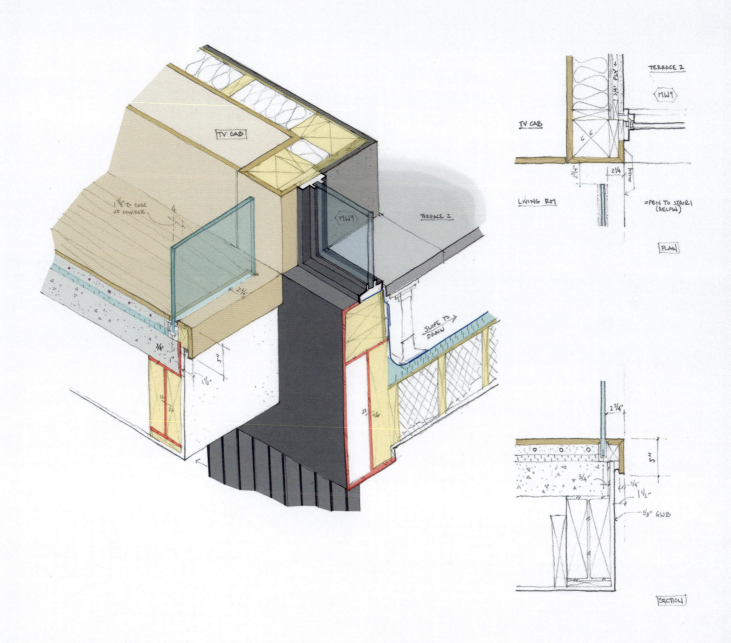

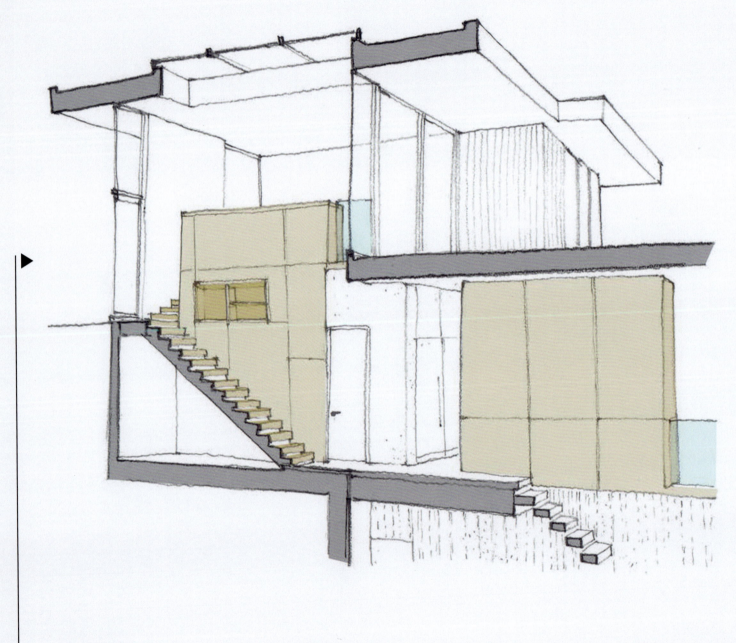

INTERIOR VIEWS

2021

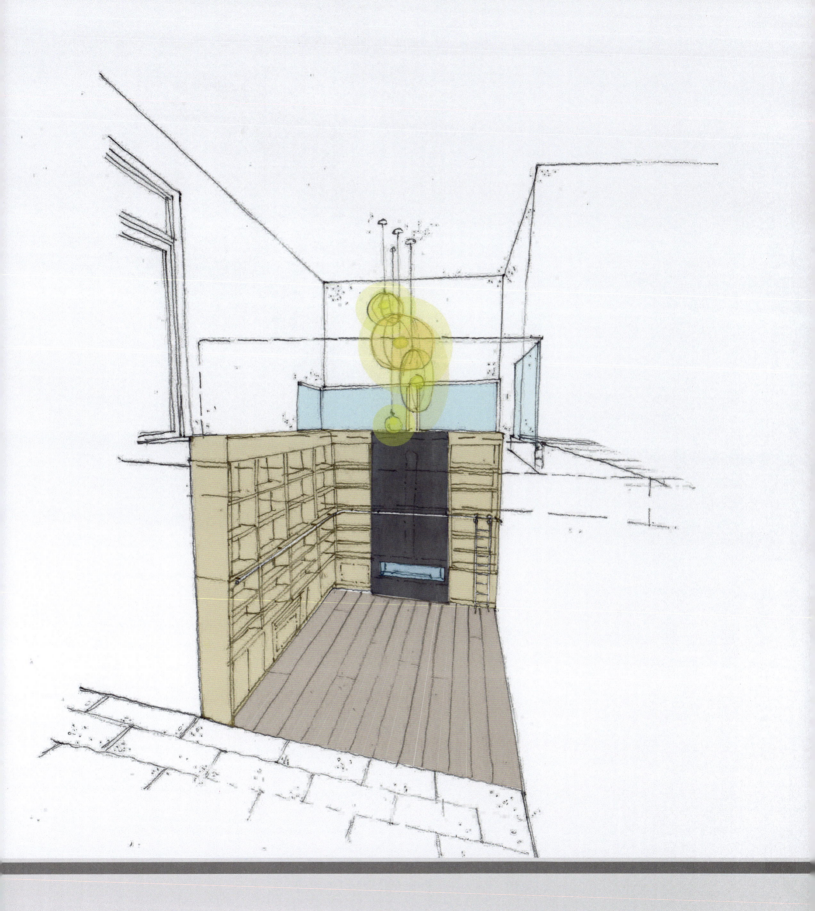

EXCAVATION AND FOUNDATION WORKS

At the initial site walk, prior to any design work, it quickly became apparent that in order for a building to work on such a steep site, a coordinated and well-thought-out approach to excavation and foundation work was essential to the success of the Terrace House. Staged earth moving and temporary shoring with soil nails up to 28 feet in length were the first construction activities required for the home to rise up and step with the land.

2021

2023

3D RENDERED VIEWS

Computer renderings are effective visual tools that not only communicate design ideas to the owner but can also maintain enthusiasm for a project during times when the permitting or construction process is moving slowly. Where hard-lined drawings and hand-drawn details illustrate how building components come together, rendered images can help visualize more clearly the finished construction.

▶ **CONSTRUCTION**
As design ideas and drawings become built reality, intentions of space and form are verified and, in some instances, adjusted to improve the building and site experience. Full-size site mockups are created for review and further selections relating to finishes, lighting, and future furnishings are made. During the construction phase not only are the plans realized but so are the outstanding decisions that still remain to be answered that will make the building a home.

2024

CONSTRUCTION (CONTINUED)
The work involved in designing a well-lit form to live within is a many-staged creative process that continues during the construction phase. With the construction of a contemporary home, the tradition of providing a meaningful attachment to a place in a specific time continues.

2024

THE OFFICE

At Mark English Architects, we believe every building we design is a prototype—the product of a specific set of circumstances. We develop every home in collaboration with the client, and in consideration of the landscape, topography, climate, and culture.

Landscape and climate play a vital role in every project, as buildings and spaces celebrate and respect their location and optimize passive solar principles. The firm draws on the California vernacular of open-plan living, light-filled spaces, and natural materials to blur the boundaries of inside and outside. Homes are embedded with a layer of artistry to reflect their residents, and every design is underscored by sustainability, with houses that are sensible, adaptable, and built to last.

Mark English, AIA, founded his eponymous practice in 1992. A Bay Area native, he offers a designer's sense of artistry supported by practical knowledge gained from years of direct, hands-on building experience.

Mark earned a Bachelor of Architecture at California Polytechnic State University, San Luis Obispo, and a Master of Architecture degree at the Syracuse University campus in Florence, Italy.

He served as a board member at AIA San Francisco (2011–2014), AIA California (2014–2016), and AIA National Small Firm Exchange (2016–2019). He has also served as a member of several design awards juries including the 2020 AIA National Small Projects Awards, 2018 AIA California Residential Design Awards, and 2013 AIASF Constructed Realities Design Awards. In addition, he is a long-time board member at the Architectural Foundation of San Francisco (AFSF) serving global elementary and secondary school students in a mentored appreciation of the AEC (architecture, engineering, and construction) process.

Mark's work has won numerous design awards including a 2024 AIASF Design Award, 2024 RD Residential Design Architecture Award, and several SARA design awards.

Mark is the editor of the respected online magazine *The Architects' Take* (thearchitectstake.com) featuring original interviews and commentary. As an early proponent of social media, he has given many presentations to the AIA and affiliated groups regarding the effective use of new media.

ACKNOWLEDGMENTS

Firstly, thank you to our clients for their commitment and bravery in undertaking one of the most important endeavors they will ever undertake. Our clients have believed in us, themselves, and our shared vision.

Over the last thirty years, our studio has remained small and always been filled with dedicated, talented architectural designers from around the world. I consider myself especially fortunate to have been working with associate Greg Corbett for the last sixteen years. Greg's consistent strength in all aspects of the practice, as well as his dry wit, have made our ever-evolving team prosper. Our current team of Greg, Corey Akers, Miti Mehta, and Simran Omer is our strongest yet.

Buildings only happen because of the work of contractors, craftspeople, and artisans. I particularly would like to thank builders Jim and Matt Daily, and Mark De Mattei for their dedication, enthusiasm, and patience. I have been fortunate to collaborate with dozens of makers over the years, and greatly acknowledge their curiosity and cleverness.

As a young person, I was intrigued by the architecture of the pueblo ruins of the American Southwest, and the wonderful work of the Inca and Maya builders in ancient America. For reasons based in culture and technology, the native builders excelled in working with the essence of the land. I'm thankful for that enduring example.

In acknowledging the pivotal role of individuals in shaping my career, I express gratitude to several key figures. Firstly, my father, Richard, who instilled in me a passion for architecture and engineering, setting high standards and offering unwavering support. Dr. Ted Ulanday, a childhood neighbor, fueled my design interests during my teenage years through his sponsorship of numerous landscape projects on his property. Mr. Bob Balcomb, my high school architecture teacher, guided me toward realizing my professional aspirations in the field. Additionally, Steven and Cathi House, my esteemed architect mentors, exemplified the essence of exceptional small-scale design.

Lastly, thank you to my wife, Jamie, who has been instrumental in my personal and professional growth, aiding me in reaching my full potential.

PROJECT CREDITS

MEADOW HOUSE   P10-39
Completed: 2023
Location: Carmel, California

MEA TEAM
Mark English
Greg Corbett
Joshua Kehl
Karli Montick
models by Waylon Ng

PROJECT TEAM
Builder: Portola Valley Builders
Structural Engineer: GFDS Engineers
Civil Engineer: Whitson Engineers
Landscape Architect: Arterra Landscape Architects
Photography: Joe Fletcher

TŌRŌ   P40-59
Completed: 2017
Location: Woodside, California

MEA TEAM
Mark English
Greg Corbett

PROJECT TEAM
Builder: Golobic Construction
Structural Engineer: Dominic Chu
Photography: Bruce Damonte

SILICON VALLEY   P60-81
Completed: 2017
Location: Silicon Valley, California

MEA TEAM
Mark English
Brian Pearson
Samantha Senn

PROJECT TEAM
Builder: De Mattei Construction
Structural Engineer: GFDS Engineers
Photography: Joe Fletcher

ATHERTON   P82-111
Completed: 2021
Location: Atherton, California

MEA TEAM
Mark English
Greg Corbett
Samantha Senn

PROJECT TEAM
Builder: De Mattei Construction
Structural Engineer: Holmes Structures
Civil Engineer: Precision Engineering and Construction Inc.
Landscape Architect: Arterra Landscape Architects
Photography: Bruce Damonte

COW HOLLOW   P112–135

Completed: 2017
Location: San Francisco, California

MEA TEAM

Mark English
Greg Corbett

PROJECT TEAM

Builder: De Mattei Construction
Structural Engineer: GFDS Engineers
Landscape Architect: Scott Lewis Landscape Architecture
Photography: Joe Fletcher

LIGHTHOUSE   P136–155

Completed: 2018
Location: Sausalito, California

MEA TEAM

Mark English
Adrienne Chen-Ok
Brian Pearson
Samantha Senn

PROJECT TEAM

Builder: Landmark Builders
Structural Engineer: GFDS Engineers
Photography: Joe Fletcher

TERRACE HOUSE   P156–175

Ongoing
Location: Woodside, California

MEA TEAM

Mark English
Greg Corbett

PROJECT TEAM

Builder: Portola Valley Builders
Structural Engineer: Holmes Structures
Shoring Engineer: American Subsurface Engineering, Inc.
Geotechnical Engineer: Romig Engineers, Inc.
Civil Engineer: Lea & Braze Engineering, Inc.
Photography: Bruce Damonte

Published in Australia in 2025 by
The Images Publishing Group Pty Ltd
ABN 89 059 734 431

Offices

MELBOURNE
Waterman Business Centre
Suite 64, Level 2 UL40
1341 Dandenong Road
Chadstone, Victoria 3148
Australia
Tel: +61 3 8564 8122

NEW YORK
6 West 18th Street 4B
New York, NY 10011
United States
Tel: +1 212 645 1111

SHANGHAI
6F, Building C, 838 Guangji Road
Hongkou District, Shanghai 200434
China
Tel: +86 021 31260822

books@imagespublishing.com
www.imagespublishing.com

Copyright © 2025 Mark English Architects (Introduction by Zahid Sardar)
The Images Publishing Group Reference Number: 1704

All plans and elevations created by Miti Mehta.
All photography is attributed in the Project Credits on pages 178–79, unless otherwise noted.
Cover and page 2: Joe Fletcher (Meadow House); page 4: Joe Fletcher (Lighthouse); page 6: Bruce Damonte (Atherton)

All rights reserved. Apart from any fair dealing for the purposes of private study, research, criticism or review as permitted under the Copyright Act, no part of this publication may be reproduced, stored in a retrieval system or transmitted in any form by any means, electronic, mechanical, photocopying, recording or otherwise, without the written permission of the publisher.

 A catalogue record for this book is available from the National Library of Australia

Title: *in Situ*: Unique Homes Crafted for California Living
Author: Mark English Architects
ISBN: 9781864709742

This title was commissioned in IMAGES' Melbourne office and produced as follows:
Creative Direction Nicole Boehringer; *Editorial* Amanda Holder, Jeanette Wall; *Production* Simon Walsh, Heather Johnson

EU GPSR Authorised Representative: Easy Access System Europe Oü
Company Registration ID: 16879218 | Address: Mustamäe tee 50, 10621 Tallinn, Estonia
Email: gpsr@easproject.com | Tel: +358 40 500 3575

Printed on 140gsm Da Dong Woodfree paper (FSC®) in China by Artron Art Group

IMAGES has included on its website a page for special notices in relation to this and its other publications.
Please visit www.imagespublishing.com

Every effort has been made to trace the original source of copyright material contained in this book. The publishers would be pleased to hear from copyright holders to rectify any errors or omissions.
The information and illustrations in this publication have been prepared and supplied by Mark English Architects. While all reasonable efforts have been made to ensure accuracy, the publishers do not, under any circumstances, accept responsibility for errors, omissions and representations, express or implied.